TAKE A LOOK  HAVE A READ

Open your mouth and
what do you see?
Your teeth!
They are small and sharp.

Your teeth play a big role! They function to cut food.

They function to chew food.

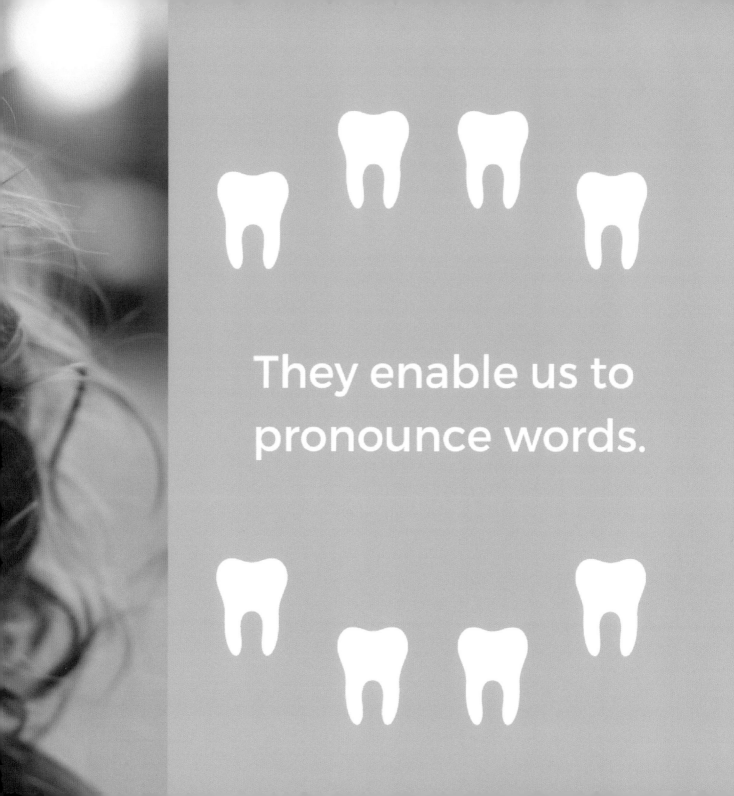

They enable us to pronounce words.

When you have strong feelings, such as fear, anger or frustration, you may want to bite.

STOP!
Small teeth do not bite!

Biting hurts!
It hurts a person's body and feelings.

When you want to bite, try doing this instead.

Drink a cup of iced juice to cool yourself down.

Chew a gummy bear candy to keep your teeth busy.

Or express your feelings in words.

Remember!
Small teeth do not bite!
Small teeth, big smile!

Printed in Great Britain
by Amazon